HYSTERIAN

poems by

Marcella Remund

Finishing Line Press
Georgetown, Kentucky

HYSTERIAN

Copyright © 2025 by Marcella Remund
ISBN 979-8-89990-093-8 First Edition
All rights reserved under International and Pan-American Copyright Conventions. No part of this book may be reproduced in any manner whatsoever without written permission from the publisher, except in the case of brief quotations embodied in critical articles and reviews.

Publisher: Leah Huete de Maines
Editor: Christen Kincaid
Cover Art: Joe Prescher www.joeprescher.com
Author Photo: Marcella Remund
Cover Design: Elizabeth Maines McCleavy

Order online: www.finishinglinepress.com
also available on amazon.com

Author inquiries and mail orders:
Finishing Line Press
PO Box 1626
Georgetown, Kentucky 40324
USA

Contents

The Midway: Opening Night 1
St. Muirgen 3
In the Time Before 4
The Axe Thrower: Gordon's Dream 5
Scent of Love 6
Golden Tightrope 7
Prayer to Boudica 8
No Space Between 9
Small Things 10
Long Track Home 12
Garage Sensei 13
Blizzard Queen 14
The Dog Boy: A Letter Home 15
Timothy Leary's Jacket 16
Cusp of Morning 17
The Open Sea 18
Zuihitsu: The Body's Unfolding 19
Caught 21
Precarious 22
The Mermaid: Lost Daughter of Doris 23
Plea to St. Paula 24
Rubaiyat: Hysterian 25
Receding into Black 26
Wild Winter 27
Bathing Mother 28
She is the Kind of Person Who 29
The Bearded Lady: Un-becoming 30
Slumber Party 32
Even the Dog is Dying 33
Zuihitsu: In Blue 34
Bipolar Firestorm 36
Snow Beasts 38
What I Try to Believe 39
The Three-legged Man: Gary's Secret 40
Motherwork 41
Diagram of Our Neglect 42

Conversation with a Friend	43
Rewilding	44
Hummingbird Moth	45
The Palm Reader: Fortune's Folly	46
The Dormition of Mother	48
Ghazal: Walking on the Edge of Night	49
St. Jeanne Jugan	50
The Fat Lady: Baby Beulah Says Yes	51
Vultures	52
Second Chance	53
Hermit's Prayer	54
The Fish Man: Neptune in the Coffee Shop	55
A Gift	57
Your Hands Tell Me Goodbye	58
Economy of Movement	59
The Tattooed Lady: Seeing Madame X for the First Time	60
Threshold	61
My Darkening Window	62
In Defense of Winter	63
The House of Glass: All the Little Hammers	64
Ghazal: Dream of the World	65
Those Nights When You Come Back	66
Plain Love Song	67
Cailleach Feasa	68
The Last Poem I'll Write	69
The Midway: Shuttering	70
Release	71
ACKNOWLEDGMENTS	72

*Midway along the journey of our life
I came to find myself in a dark wood,
for I had wandered off from the straight path.*

*How hard it is to tell what it was like,
this wood of wilderness, savage and stubborn
(the thought of it brings back all my old fears),*

*a bitter place! Death could scarce be bitterer.
But if I would show the good that came of it
I must talk about things other than the good.*

Dante Alighieri, Inferno, Canto I

THE MIDWAY: Opening Night

> *After the end of the world*
> *after my death*
> *I found myself in the middle of life*
> *creating myself...*
>
> Tadeusz Różewicz

From a block or two off, all you see are lights
and flashes. Your pupils pin, you tilt your head
so the good ear catches the high-striker bell

and organ-grinder honk and whine. Your mouth
already tastes like cotton candy. Closer now,
you get a whiff of elephant shit and maybe

a little what? frying cheese? beer vomit? You slow
down but can't stop moving toward those lights.
Soon, you're smack in the middle of the Midway.

Hawkers on both sides lean out, call your name,
tempt you with nostalgia—*Win this ballerina doll/*
Care Bear/My Little Pony/unicorn! Step right up!

You dig in a pocket, but you're broke. You cross
the street and beg a funnel cake, look back wistfully
at your old neighborhood, the dimming glow

of streetlights fuzzy, prettier than you remember.
You can't go back to those familiar shadows.
Movement farther down the street, a few booths

past the Tilt-O-Whirl, catches your eye. A woman
bends over a cane, gums a corndog. Beyond
her, past the lights and bells, past clowns on stilts,

popping kettle corn, the rank pacing tigers,
the grate & grind of a Ferris wheel, past toothless
carnies, swayback ponies, the street disappears

in pitch black. Nowhere to go for now.
You pull a shawl close around your shoulders
and slow to a shuffle, stranded on the Midway.

ST. MUIRGEN

patron of mermaids

Lí Ban, such sad romance in your finned tail,
your skin half silk, half scale, brethren salmon
slick and cold against you. I don't wonder

that you and your otter-dog found surviving
the flood more bearable in the company of eel,
bladderwort and sponge. How long did you,

king's daughter, long for your village, for your
straw bed and fire, for dry air, for the touch
of creatures warm with pumping blood?

You were so long in the water, did your fins
stiffen with age, your tail arthritic, hair a tangle
of algae and pondweed, your scales brittle

and broken off among the hornwort tangles?
When after 300 years Béoán heard you sing,
fished you out, did you choose the baptism

just to lie on the sand where you could see sky
once more? Did you know the air would kill you,
that the price of heaven would be your magic?

Lí Ban, St. Muirgen, take away my longing
for the deep, for the lullaby of the sea. Bless me
with held breath, with the music of trees and stones.

IN THE TIME BEFORE

In the time before, when fontanelles
        were still open, I moved easily between
                body and *There*, like moving between
                        a small closet and an endless wild garden.

In the time before, Beloved, we recognized each other
        by the pulsing signatures of our heartlights,
                the timbre of waves and frequencies,
                      the reach of rays.

So much from the time before
        is gauzy memory now, quick pictures
                that roll past just before sleep, like
                        loose film reels left to spin, flap.

I wake feeling the warm wrap of your thighs
        There—were dark and light the same *There*?
                Did I see a cat sleeping on a chiseled stone?
                      Was I singing, holding you, you holding me?

In this time of yellowed paper, fading pictures, dust,
        let us keep a toe in the doorway, keep the way
                clear so together, we can make our way
                      back *There*, home to the time before.

THE AXE THROWER: Gordon's Dream

Behind the elephant tent, Gordon grinds
down the blade of an axe until it feels
like a beveled windowpane. It will leave
a wicked bruise, he knows, if it hits her.

Better a bruise or broken bone at worst,
than the fate (hers and his alike) he sees
in his dream each night, rousing him in
flop sweats, heart firing like a machine gun.

Loretta has sewn a loop in the purple silk
lining of his cape, and he has mastered
a slight-of-hand swap, bladed axe
for bludgeon, so one lucky paying

customer can test the blade, split a piece
of paper on the razor's edge. Loretta
is still so beautiful in her fringed leotard,
platinum hair piled in a beehive, purple

and gold sash to match her blindfold,
hands on her hips. They met when both
were bored Nebraska teens. Now, since
his stroke, Gordon feels age twist

his muscles, untether tendons, pop
and loosen aching joints. He's given up
coffee, but still the tremors in his hands,
still the jolting dream, the waking panic.

As he lines up Loretta against a glittering
rainbow target and kisses her, he knows—
it's a matter of time. It's only
a matter of time.

SCENT OF LOVE

We have learned each other, Beloved—
surface tension, geography and slope

of back and jutting hip, geometry of
more delicate, deliberate sex, addition

and subtraction of tenderness. Most of all,
we have come to know, without reasoning,

our cauldron of smell—witch's brew
of nostalgia, desire, devotion, its chasm

of joy and sorrow into which we fall again
and again and are stirred together, our flesh

and bone stewed in the spices of us, this new
steam filling both our lungs. I understand now

why a widow keeps a husband's work shirt
and boots neat in the closet, why she goes

to the closet daily to caress button and collar,
press sleeve to cheek, close her eyes.

How is it your smell alone makes me cry?
How, when you're away, does your pillow

held to my breast thread its gossamer
inside me, spin me into dreamy sleep?

Here we are, my beloved, beyond the
sudden fires, the explosions and tumult

of our beginnings, in this new world
of instinct and cell memory, where

even milk-eyed I could find you, where
a deep breath is a perfect act of love.

GOLDEN TIGHTROPE

I am the golden child suspended, caught
midpoint on my golden wire, still tucking
up my childish feet to keep them from
the hot lava. On an island below, my father

at 90 calls out to me. (Finally!) Regrets
are eating through his soft tissues
(heart, eyes, brain's squishy memories)
even faster than the prostate cancer that

swims upriver in his bone marrow. Death
stands beside him, their elbows hooked,
my father regretting now his covenant,
his bargain with Jesus, for 100 years.

On another island, my mother's fear
of oblivion sparks little fires that blacken
the soles of my feet. I once hoped
they'd burn off her blood's cancer,

boil it clean (a miracle of terror), but
they only char my skin to ash layer
by layer. At 85 now, she calls my name
over and over and over. But when I look

down, she sees in me only a mirror,
imperfect replica. Death watches
her too, waves to catch her eye. She
turns her back, pretends not to notice.

My brothers do all they can, hold
the wire tight, but they're my parents'
happy toys, the fun uncles. Mine are
the toes curled around the wire,

the riven clinging hands I use to swing
from island to island, measure morphine,
scrub toilets, powder paper skin, dress
wounds, put out lights, floods, flames.

PRAYER TO BOUDICA

Boudica, no saint surely but hero
or hysterian, I light this flame
for you. When your husband died,

his Roman guests quickly turned.
The pillagers whipped you, raped
your daughters in front of you, stole

your kingdom. I don't wonder that
you took up the sword, left charity
behind. You must have stunned

your enemies, red-maned lioness
storming northward, no mercy for
woman or child, ox or goat, Roman

heads for the pikes to show you meant
business. Your victories—a widowed
woman's victories—must have left

Roman mouths agape, until they woke
from their stupor and finally defeated
your army. And it must have

frustrated soldiers aching to impale
you, that you even chose your own
end, swallowed the poison.

Boudica, I'm an aging lioness, thorn
in my paw, no warrior queen. Let me
touch my tongue to your rage, let me

warm at your iron heart's fire, let me
feel your muscles twist and tighten in me.
Help me—limping, stooped sometimes—
to stand always on my own two feet.

NO SPACE BETWEEN

Here in the middle, time overlaps, folds in on itself. It is possible here for two objects to occupy the same space. For a butcher knife, let's say, with a carved walnut stock, to lie in moldering leaves beneath the footpath of a mouse, for the mouse to leave a skittering blood trail of dots & dashes across the knife's broad blade, and for the mouse to be gone before you register movement. Or, for light from a crack in Venetian blinds to illuminate the rim of a deep urn into which someone has poured the coarse, uneven ash that was once your dog or cat or father, and for the light and dark to leave their imprint on your retina in the microsecond before your brain senses the perfect paradox and you, in joy and sorrow, begin to weep. Or, for a man to be pulled constantly inward so tightly, so silently, that the core of him is gathered into a solid ball at once contracting and radiant, for that man to occupy the same space as a woman pulled outward, stretched like carnival taffy into scalloped ribbons that ripple and fold in air currents, then double back around the man, a woman softened almost to melting by his golden heat.

SMALL THINGS

When she
was a child,
they called
her dwarf,
midget,
Lilliputian.
They liked
how she fit
in a hamper,
how small,
how far away
her voice
sounded.
They liked
the peach of
her face, her
tiny ears,
hands, feet.
They dressed
her in pink
petticoats,
cowgirl outfits
with lariats,
gold lamé
princess gowns
with matching
wands. She
was their
life-sized,
squeezable
doll.

Once she began
to grow into her body's idea
of itself, they called her chunky, round.
They called out her child-bearing hips, her
back fat, her thunder thighs, her tree-trunk legs.
They told her drink less, starve, work harder, runrunrun.
Then her wrinkles, dimples, creases, sags. Her pouches, pillows.

Even when her hair turned white, they stared as she filled her plate,
furrowed their brows at potatoes, smiled at steamed butterless beans,
stood guard over cakes and pies. They scowled at her girth,
tamped her volume, feared she could not be contained

LONG TRACK HOME

Below the bluff and west along the Vermillion River,
the 10:45 train blows its whistle, one quick burst.

Faint at first, it's my childhood calling from a backyard,
where I'm in my underpants, shining a flashlight

into the dark peak of a blanket tent, singing "Mairzy Doats,"
so brave and so scared. I'm a city block from the tracks.

The train whistle is my grandmother's last sigh
before snoring on nights she lets me crawl in her bed.

It's a church organ chord played *tenuto*. It's the midnight
angel's accordion lullaby, rocking me to sleep.

Back here above the bluff, far from my childhood,
the train crosses into town, its whistles closer together,

more insistent. Somewhere, deer springboard into the trees.
Wheels scrape steel tracks, raise the hair on my arms.

If I lie very still, I feel the train rumble through
the floorboards, up the legs of our bedframe, and into

my spine. She's there, I find her again—child in a tent,
her flashlight shining out now from my half-closed eyes,

the organ playing a hymn I so want to believe in,
the midnight angel's accordion lulling me to sleep.

GARAGE SENSEI

When my father practiced judo and karate
spring and summer in the garage, winter

in the basement, I got to ride along. He
built a base, a square of railroad ties

with a vertical kick post, a two-by-four
padded with foam rubber and duct tape.

He put a kid on each side to steady the base,
keep it from jumping across the cement

with each kick or punch. The four of us
took turns. We stood on the ties and held

on to the post. The jolt from his strikes
shook up through my chicken legs and

sometimes knocked me on the floor,
laughing until I was out of breath.

Afterward, he would soak in a hot bath
until he fell asleep. Sometimes,

my mother snuck in and pulled the plug
to let the sudden cold at him, her quiet

punishment for one betrayal or another.
Later, he would pay me a quarter for

every fifteen minutes I scratched his back
during *Sing Along with Mitch* or *Dragnet*.

Now that he's gone, I skip over memories
of holes he punched in the wall, phone books

torn in half to stop a sibling squabble, years
he disappeared without a word. Instead,

I skip back to the garage where, in pigtails and bare
feet, I bow to my sensei and hang on for dear life.

BLIZZARD QUEEN

Driving at night along South Dakota
highways, we watch hypnotic snow
come down like all the world's

confetti. These first fat flakes mean
the snow's half-hearted—wet enough
for snowball fights, it melts into ditch

rivers as it hits the ground. But small
flakes mean *don't leave home!*
Those flakes are dry, serious—they

pile up, stick around till spring,
fuzz focus, drift high as doorknobs.
Small flakes mean check the larder,

stack wood to last through April,
dig out candles and books, brew strong
coffee, give each other a wide berth.

You and I are out here tonight, fools
in our clown car convinced the show
must go on, when Blizzard Queen

swings down on her Coteau des Prairie
trapeze, tosses back wild white hair,
spits her tiniest flakes like circus glitter.

THE DOG BOY: A Letter Home

Danny wets the hair on the back of his hand,
slicks it down, puts a cartridge in the pen and
starts a letter to Anichka. He tells her they're

halfway through the season, somewhere in Kansas.
He'll have a nine-hour day tomorrow—nine hours
to prowl the stage, bare porcelain fangs, howl, pick

a front-row girl to charge and make her scream.
He tells Anichka about fields of sunflowers
so like Marchuk's *Tenderness*, about unbroken

flatland miles that lull him to dreamless sleep,
about Ellison's *Invisible Man* tearing his heart
in two. He signs the letter *Yours alone, Danya*

with a little heart. He folds it, kisses and seals it
in an envelope, presses it in a cigar box in his
dressing table with so many others.

In the mirror, he
combs in mascara to hide
his muzzle's grey streak.

TIMOTHY LEARY'S JACKET

The day Timothy Leary showed up
in Vegas, black & white checked jacket
like a nuclear test pattern, I trembled.
He pulled me through the air, along an
invisible trail, wave of his spidery hand.

Pied piper of hypnotic near-reason,
his tweaked melody once smoked me
out of town to strange new lands with
vaporous borders, lava lamps, sweaty
sex passed off as love and never free.

Dying by then, thin as a windowpane,
he smirked, teased with death-talk, studied
my eyes—curious prankster watching
to see if I would still drift along, re-light
his candle, un-toe his imaginary line.

I might have followed again, old as I am
(drawn by cell memory or acid flashback),
but long ago I had dropped back in, felt
the fire of waking life, and no ice cold
demigod can smother these flames now.

CUSP OF MORNING

In those moments when I float and drift
near the open door of dreams, somewhere

between a locked iron gate so tall I can't
make out its finials among clouds, and the home

of my youth, eternally on fire but without
ash or cinder, I hear a voice half singing,

Wake, dear one, wake! But I roll my eyes
back in my head, turn onto my side and keep

dreaming, curious to see who else comes to warm
themselves at the flames, or what three-toed

creatures climb the gate and disappear in the clouds,
in a sky that shifts just now, whooshes below

my feet as I lift sudden wings, tilt my head
just so, and bank toward a sliver of moon.

THE OPEN SEA

My mother's slow, steady breathing is
my lighthouse beacon—sail on, seas
are safe! Her open mouth signals she's
asleep, I can exhale at last, drop anchor.

Half in my bunk, I risk closing my eyes,
diving into brief rest, but avast! She has not
made peace with her first mate, Death.
Any sound could wake her, could mean

Death is trying again to pry her hands
loose from the guardrail she grips even
sound asleep, the rail that keeps her safe
aboard this hospital bed, her funeral ship.

Each time she wakes, I wake, weigh
anchor, set sail again. Over and over
I steer toward the sunset, as if the
horizon was not the edge of the world.

Zuihitsu: THE BODY'S UNFOLDING

In my lower spine, remnants of pavement and gravel from a bike wreck. If I stand too long at the Walmart checkout, ice water burns down the nerves of my right leg, my own portable lightning.

A genetic mutation to the protein MC1R in 2% of us produces red pheomelanin instead of black, turning hair red. It makes redheads feel pain differently—we're less afraid of needles, more susceptible to hot and cold. We need more anesthesia. We're more impervious to electric shock. Some still think we're vampires.

We should get a badge, sewn roughly on a cotton sash, for each passage: titanium joint, pig heart valve, stroke survival, Teflon stent, dentures, hysterectomy, pacemaker, cancer surgery's slow dissection, those softly whooshing machines that keep us breathing at night.

Some rooms in sleep, not even the shrill cries of children can reach.

This is how I know the mind and body have a loose connection: My body gladly gives in to gravity, daily wear, disruption, weathering, breakage, dissolution. But in my mind, I still knot a sweater around the monkey bars and swing by my knees.

Somewhere in an old journal—dreams of magical creatures rubbing against my leg, skies opening like great arched doorways, God's voice saying, *eat the entire kumquat, peel and all.*

I once lived on brown rice, cabbage, and soybean sprouts for a month. I ate one meal a day, a bowlful with hot bean paste. I gained three pounds. Every day since has been some new kind of starvation—new eating plan, new drug, new 5-day fast, new walking program, new lifestyle change, new rejection of a tender and careful lover, new battle plan for ambushing my enemy fat. I tell you, I can pile it on, so strong is my body's instinct for survival. When my therapist asked if I'd ever considered self-harm, I answered *NO* without hesitation.

Our joints are shark skeleton, hyaline cartilage like window glass stretched over porous bone. We're such flexible and terribly breakable things.

The first child came straight through my belly—vertical door carved through layers of skin, fat, muscle, then shut with dozens of heavy black sutures tied like macramé knots. The second child came through the same door, scalpeled open again, reshaped, closed with stitches clear as cat-gut. The third too came through this way, the doorframe planed and trimmed, closed and locked for good with a staple gun.

Suddenly, the hand holding this book is not my own. You'd know it if you saw it, wouldn't you?

Ice cold peaches sliced
into crescent boats sail on
a still-wild sea of tongue.

CAUGHT

It's best to forget.
        Forget the way the bruise-blue
                spreads under your skin

like seeping seawater, like a cluster
        of bluebells wilting in late afternoon.
                Forget each day's constant clanging—

the news, death counts, digging in
        behind new enemy lines, friends
                turned strangers, their mouths full

of burnt slogans. Forget that fear
        was let go from its cage, how it stalks
                you, fanged, gone feral, how it steals

newborns. Forget pleasantries,
        kindness, long embraces. Forget
                nostalgia always biting at your heels.

Forget all traces of the time before.
        In fact, it's best to forget
                the whole year, decades even, today.

Forget the constant unraveling
        of the beautiful sticky webs
                we've spent our lives spinning,

and in which we've only caught
        ourselves, having long forgotten
                how to bite through the silk.

PRECARIOUS

Shot full of gadolinium contrast dye and lying on my radioactive bed, I feel my heart miss another beat, pause for dramatic effect, then *glug* back to life in a backwash thud so hard it rattles my ribs. Today, everything about me is an arabesque en pointe, pirouette on the point of a fine-gauge needle, balanced on a wire the thickness of a human hair, stretched to near breaking across a gaping chasm. That my heart beats at all leaves me so stymied, I ask for another warm blanket. I glide inside the great machine, lights and whirs a symphony of uncertainty that lulls me almost to sleep. I should be claustrophobic, but instead I feel safely contained by tomography, mapping the topography of this foreign land, each organ sliced and held in place, fragile beads on some god's mala. The small black spot on my lung is the Guru bead that must not be touched. Most days this body trusts its auto-pilot, its sparking neurons, muscle fibers, electric pulses, chemical signals, biophysics. But today, it's all invisible rays, droning chants, plants from a prehistoric witches' herbal that bubble in a cauldron of magic beans, and something that once was me, cut into floating pieces that ribbon through a spinning void.

THE MERMAID: Lost Daughter of Doris

I'm most alive in the tank, cradled
in shifting ribbons of saltwater,
safe from gawkers and their bleating,

their faces distorted, comical. The only
sound is the song-hum of the pump,
its thin tube hidden among the stones

and drifting plants. But I scarcely
need to breathe air now. Not half of a
monkey skeleton stitched to a fish tail

(that was Barnam's monster). No, my
feet and ankles webbed from birth,
I am miracle daughter of Doris, nymph

goddess of the sea. On land, I'm clumsy,
dried up and dull, ordinary as they are.
But in the water! A silver trident

and jeweled crown, my floating breasts,
scales like blue-green mirrors, some
boy's 25-cent minnow tossed in, caught

and flicking between my teeth, I'm
spectacle—reaching for them, graceful,
smiling, unforgettable, terrifying.

PLEA TO ST. PAULA

patron of wives and widows

St. Paula, my sisters and I, though stippled
with blue veins, stoved up by frozen joints,
blinking behind bifocals thick as leaded

windows, are too young to knuckle under.
There must be some final reward for these
long years of battle or service, labor or love.

Some of our helpmates have long since
slunk off with firm-breasted women, some
have taken that rocky road home, leaving us

widowed. Help us to breathe deeply, release
twisted muscles, to be only ourselves again.
Bless us, St. Paula, with knees that still fold

into a kayak, with eyes sharp enough to follow
pages into astonishing new worlds, with
arms like Atlas to bear this weight of aging.

Help us to be companion and comfort for
each other when in each of our homes, evening
fires burn down and rooms echo with stillness.

Rubaiyat: HYSTERIAN

She melts into the scenery, until
she's a foreground fog against a hill.
She's losing substance, disappearing.
Soon she'll be a blur gone still.

Sometimes she remembers being seen—
bright flame burning hot between
red waterbed sheets, then cooling, cool, until
the flame became a wisp of steam.

Most see just a shopping cart
wheel itself past box wine at Walmart,
or feel the breeze-flap of her bingo arms,
or hear the slow beating of her heart.

She loves that she can finally wear
stripes and plaid with sapphire hair.
She loves that she can stomp, scream,
rant on, and no one seems to care.

Still, transparency can be lonely,
and though she laughs it off, she's only
human, pack animal like all the rest,
longing to be visible now and then, known.

It's not the disused, has-been womb
erasing her, or the general gloom
of modern life—it's the gaping mouth
we recognize behind her, that open tomb.

RECEDING INTO BLACK

after Web, Allan D'Arcangelo (U.S., 1979)

In the foreground of D'Arcangelo's *Web*,
two solid beams form an X, joined
in the center by a wrap, a bow, something
uncertain, pliable, like heart muscle between
ribs. The beams are maroon, with sunburned

red scaffolding behind, crisscrossed, angular
veins against a grey building. The scaffold
could be metal, glints like metal in a trick
of light. We study each other this way too,
you and I, trying to see all the intersections,

size up each other's inner workings according
to outward structures, measure each other
only by what catches the light. What if
scaffolds have cores of thick sticky liquid
running the length of each beam, centers

that soften to liquid in the heat? Under
the building's eaves in the painting, an
unformed test swatch of exuberant orange.
Could this be disguise? A face to mask our
tenderness, to scare and scatter? And what

are we to make of the sky, its painful blue
a thumbed nose at everything below it?
Behind and below the web of bolts and beams,
in the building's darkened doorway, we
cower—older, shriveled, receding into black.

WILD WINTER

Yesterday on the South Dakota prairie,
our ground cover of red and brown leaves
ruffled and bug-bitten, was dusted with winter's

pollen, a layer of snow downy as a hare's
winter coat. Now the wind picks up, an invisible
hand grates glaciers into icy shavings over the

great bowl of buffalo grass and bluestem.
Tangle mosses turn to snowcones on trees'
north sides. We go feral, evolution in reverse,

dig our way back inside our den. We circle
the bedroom, paw at blankets, curl together,
settle. After six months of furnace hum,

overgrown nails, and living on fat stores, crocus
and squill will push up. We'll smell new green,
stretch, shake ourselves loose—human again.

BATHING MOTHER

The first time I bathed Mother
after the cancer's blade carved the great
mountain of her (one I could never approach)

into a rutted hill of loose flesh and jutting
bone, I noticed for the first time the odd
angle of one rib, where some minute fracture—

falling against the bed post, leaning too hard
into a kitchen chair, or breathing—had dented
an otherwise smooth arc. I traced the rib

with a soapy hand, gently washed her back.
This new land! There, behind her knee,
a scar like a ragged star. Below her

disappearing breasts, a curtain of skin
where cancer had eaten up the muscle
and fat. The discoveries of this moment,

my mother soaked and naked, small,
afraid to look me in the eyes, was
something beyond intimacy. It was

mystery unveiling itself, it was a gasp
without sound, her final unspoken question
for me, one I will never be able to answer.

SHE IS THE KIND OF PERSON WHO

She was not quite what you would call refined;
she was not quite what you would call unrefined.
She was the kind of person who keeps a parrot.
    Mark Twain

In the photo, my great-grandmother Effie
stands in a dirt yard, spring or fall maybe,
against a leafless tree. She stands with heavy

arms folded across her breast, striped cotton
dress falling to just above thick ankles, dark
hair cropped close. Her broad face, double chin,

pendulous brow and wide nose belong on a
sailor or logger, that jolly smile from Sunday's
drink behind the shed. In the background,

someone's front porch beyond a dusty maze
of pre-sidewalk paths between neighbors,
shrubs and patchy grass newly emerging

or burnt to grey already by summer. And here
my great-gran speaks to me from the creased
paper, she and I the same age in this frozen moment:

On her shoulder, a white dish towel. On the towel
a fat parrot sits, tilts its head, stares into the camera,
the two of them so at ease with each other.

Perched just now on the back of a kitchen chair,
my grey parrot Stella cocks her head, eyes
the picture too, calls out my name.

THE BEARDED LADY: Un-becoming

i.

Soon after Louise dropped out of high school
at 17, pregnant with the first of five (the
father a dock worker who would leave her
for a tanned teen waitress before the last

child arrived), she plucked a long red hair
from her jawline. By 27, tweezers clanked
in her pockets. Her youngest twisted stray
chin hairs in his fat fingers as he nursed.

At 35, Louise took to shaving daily,
face, arms, legs, the oldest daughter
got her back, their public-housing flat
ripe with soiled sheets, sour milk, Noxema.

A loaf of Wonder bread, a jar of mayo,
a block of government cheese sat out. Kids
ran past, gouged out cheese hunks. Louise
waitressed nights at Big Bob's while

the kids watched TV, fought, slept. She
read out back in the quiet alley on break.
At 45, the kids flown like autumn starlings,
Louise lost her job cleaning airport toilets.

She turned invisible, transparent. Who
would hire now a stubble-chinned, see-
through woman? The cash ran out, the
fridge emptied. Louise stopped shaving.

ii.

At 48, Louise passed Mickey outside
a strip mall bar. He turned his head,
smiled, looked her in the eyes. He didn't
look away, fidget, kick the pavement.

Each morning now, her robe draped
in loose layers, she sips coffee, sits
at a lighted mirror, puts on lipstick,
shapes her beard into a broad scallop.

She kneads in mousse, scrunches her beard
into waves, ties it with ribbon. She pulls
a satin dress over Spanx, steps into
rhinestone heels. Mickey's gone already,

taking tickets. Later, in a tent near the Fun
House, Louise shines under a spotlight,
sits in a wingback chair, legs crossed.
Rhinestones dangle from one foot, flash

in the light. She reads Browning today,
to whispering women, men with caught
tongues, kids who point and gape. She
poses for pictures. Mickey counts the take.

Tonight they'll settle in, eat roast
and new potatoes. Her kids will bring
the babies to visit later this summer, and
everyone, *everyone* can see her now.

SLUMBER PARTY

> *Agnes sweet, and Agnes fair,*
> *Hither, hither, now repair;*
> *Bonny Agnes, let me see*
> *The lad who is to marry me.*
>   *Traditional St. Agnes Eve Song*

Our granddaughters are awake, St. Agnes, in Keats'
  honey'd middle of the night, his *lambs*
    unshorn not too subtle a metaphor, really,

for the virgins they are. And why, we wonder,
  did you martyr yourself at thirteen only to
    become an old shepherd who leads these girls,

your flock, to the wolves? Why protect them
  all the way to the marriage chutes,
    where men's blades will cleave them in two?

Why pull them from the frying-pan gaze
  of men's desire just to render them in the fire
    of wedding nights? We grandmothers

are teaching our children a new song, Agnes.
  Soon they will not sing to you. Instead, they will
    wave spears, embrace each other, pick
      grey ticked fur from their baby teeth.

EVEN THE DOG IS DYING

and I'm failing this latest test
of my *be here now* mettle. I stare
out the window at Winter's dark

stubbled hills and wonder why
something, anything, can't be
permanent. Or maybe this is the

revelation of landfill plastics
and diapers—hotels for post-
humanity cockroaches. Beside

me on the bed, the dog shudders
in his sleep when I feel the tumor
on his foot and wonder where—

spine, liver, spleen—the cancer
has sent its invading armies, what
soft tissues they occupy now,

displacing, pillaging, subjugating
his native cells. How can I be One
with so much war? Across the room,

My mother sleeps too, a generator's
wheezeclank spilling its useless
oxygen into her, as if air alone
is enough to keep us here.

Zuihitsu: IN BLUE

There's something dichotomous about bachelor buttons—the frill of fringed petals, bright lapis, each bloom's golden eye, spindly stems going up and up. They are too flamboyant, too delicate, too surprising to button up a bachelor. They belong vased on a woman's dresser scarf instead, punctuating in blueblueblue her quiet suspension midway across life's highwire.

Just beneath my freckled skin, a roadmap of blue veins carry used-up blood back to the heart and lungs—powerhouse central. Pumped full of oxygen again, arteries take their fresh load back down interstate speedways, gravel roads, alleys, then cloverleaf around organs to dump off the good red stuff. Sometimes, I want to hush all this noise so I can hear the highway's hum.

Blue has the second shortest wavelength humans can see.
450-495 nanometres.
Violet is first but too royal.
On the color wheel, blue is the creek between green cattail rushes and violet phlox.
Across the wheel, blue's complement orange spills off, into my hair.

She stares out the car window, wonders why flickering sunlight through the trees' passing canopy feels so painful today—jackhammer cracking behind her eyes. Or why the bumpknot texture of her grandmother's crocheted afghan makes her cry. Today, her world folds in on itself behind a blue veil, gets small, hard to see, indistinct. The car speeds up.

Dive into the sea, down where turquoise turns cobalt/ash/blackest black, where lungs must breathe a new kind of air, where strange creatures grow their own headlamps and swim off, leave you dog paddling in the dark. Here you'll begin to understand silence in the familiar way of the womb. Keep a goggled eye on the gauges, though, because soon you'll want to stay.

There are 260 kinds of blue. There's a blue for each of us, blues with their own names or braided into words like

baptista
        lupine
                hollow
                        perfect sky
                                bruise
                                          hopeless
                                                  vein

Blue is directive, instructive, seductive, destructive—the river's winding passage on a painted map, the Blue Devil acetylene torch, $49.99. I want to love the blue, to twist my fingers into its weave instead of always, always, trying to shake it off. But

there are two hundred
sixty kinds of blue, and these
are just the colors.

BIPOLAR FIRESTORM

When the door opens and I know I'm going in,
I'll try to warn you. You should run, hide. Hold on
to something solid. Close your eyes. Keep your

head down. If you stay, you will be wrong about
a small thing at first, then another thing, then
whatever careful gesture you make will be

wrongwrongwrong. Don't kid yourself; I'll mean
every word—I'll be searching for blame,
for tinder. You will be nearest and so easily lit.

My temporary toxic neuro-swill will force open
time's neatly labeled files, drag everything
you've ever done, every oddly-angled facial

expression, every pause (read *neglect*) into
the roaring flames I can't stop fanning,
where even your kindest words will explode

between us like 4th-of-July M80s. I'll turn to
you, weep, heave until my breathing stops.
I won't care how scared you are. I'll see you

there, but I'll be seeing everything then through
a grey scrim that covers my vision like fog, like
chiffon tentacles. My tongue will turn razor blade,

I'll have trouble closing my lips around it without
blood. When sleep grabs me in a chokehold, I'll
collapse at last, face buried in a pillow. I'll shudder

and sigh for an hour or two, you wide awake,
trembling beside me. Somewhere in fitful dreams
of barred doors, constant flapping of clothes

on a line, abandoned children left in my care,
the switch will finally flip. My breath will even out,
yours will come back to you in a quiet gasp. You

are so strong, so brave, Beloved. When they say
how lucky we are, it's okay to tell them you live
sometimes in a firestorm, with scars to prove it.

SNOW BEASTS

The snow started just after dusk. Someone was scattering
armloads of silver glitter over the edges of clouds, and it
floated down into the streetlight glow. She tightroped along
the curb, dressed only in a paisley nightgown and red wool mittens.

She danced to the middle of the street and spun, head back,
tongue out, until she was a kaleidoscope of textures and colors,
red hands dusted with diamonds. Snow fell through the night.
She had gone back in for her blue coat and boots, and now

she was sitting atop a drift that had sculpted itself against the trunk
of an Ash next door. She was poised on the crest of the drift, frozen
blue dolphin on a crushed-ice wave, leaning back to look up at the
falling tinsel in the moonlight. She was half hidden in snow-speckled

light and the tree's moon shadows. I could hear her singing.
I watched her from my living room window, wrapped in a shawl,
cat stalking the sofa back, with all the lights off. She was like
a dream of softly stirring color, a glorious painting unfolding itself

on the white canvas of snow's static. I rested my tired head
on the back of the sofa, wanted to be her, tried not to blink.
The cat kneaded my thigh, circled and curled in. The wind
picked up, orchestra for her lullaby. The snow stopped

four days later. Our flat street had turned wild countryside
of white hills and deep valleys. The whole street busied itself
digging out from under the drifts, moving muscles stiff
from too much sleep. I watched the neighbors' houses for her,

decided she'd been a snow vision brought on by faltering eyes
or tricks of winter light. I felt a hollow in my chest where I kept
an ache for her. I may have wept. Weeks later, in the grey
slush of melting, a spring squirrel spotted paisley and dug.

WHAT I TRY TO BELIEVE

On Tuesdays, the hospice nurse strips
you, Mother, bathes you in the hospital
bed set adrift in your bedroom.

The nurse wraps a warm cloth around
your chin, spa-like, washes under
wrinkled folds where muscles once

rose and fell. She lifts each of your
hands so tenderly, enfolds them in her
own, smooths in April Spring lotion.

She trims and paints your nails, gently
powders your paper skin, diapers you,
slips you in a nightgown cut open

up the back to the collar, until you sink
again, so small, into your bed of flannel
roses. I have time those days to eat,

wash dishes, shower, fold laundry, but
all I can do is hold my breath, blink,
stare into your glassy eyes and that

nurse's patient smile. *You're so lucky,*
the nurse always says, and every
Tuesday, Mother, I try to believe her.

THE THREE-LEGGED MAN: Gary's Secret

Women love to set their squealing infants
in Harold's lap, $2 for a photo of terrified
baby on the "Three-legged Human Chair."

Gawkers don't know the extra leg, a fourth
tiny foot taped tight to his thigh, and the
extra bone that widens Harold's flowering

pelvis, is his faceless twin, his remnant
brother. Harold calls him Gary. For two
shows nightly, he and Gary take turns kicking

a football across the stage to Harold's wife,
Phyllis. Who wills Gary's third foot to kick
is circus magic, mystery. Arthritis slows

and stiffens Harold's odd angles now, but
he still sneaks curious young women into an
empty tent if they hound him, beg a closer look.

Each time, Phyllis calls him "three-timer,"
makes him sleep outside, but she knows—
women can't resist Gary's hidden charms.

MOTHERWORK

Down on the flats along the river,
a turkey hen flutters open great wings
above a late spring brood, umbrella

against the coming rain. She tucks,
nestles chicks under shiver-spread
breast feathers, until all eight disappear.

The hen alerts, goes silent, statue-still
as whiskers flick past, noses and noisy
feet press flat the brome as a line

of chittering raccoons moves beyond
the hen, skitters for the water's edge.
She has saved her young once again.

But there are so many hungry mouths
this time of year, so many mothers
scouting and sniffing to feed their own.

The hen settles, presses her body low
into weeds and dirt. She rests now, eyes
half open. Like mothers everywhere,
she knows any truce is temporary.

DIAGRAM OF OUR NEGLECT

Let Y be the number of chances,
the millennia we've had to get it right,
let's say since monkeys first climbed
down, stood, took up pointed sticks.

Let X be the slowly shrinking size
of our hearts, from super-pumped primate
pounders, to fear-shriveled human nuggets,
to the coming scrap-heap of nuts & bolts.

Call the point of origin the Big Bang,
Creation, Cartesian Center, Sucking
Void of Dark Matter, the Great
Whatever, the Big Fat Zero.

Now shade in the portion of our graph
that signifies homeless teens, pregnant
women in prison, dead school children,
monkeys gone hairless, sticks gone guns.

Watch as the shaded section seeps,
spreads like spear-in-the-side plasma
on litmus, until the whole graph is
fulvous, smeared, warped and buckled.

Then set a match to it, because really,
who wants to see the trajectory, the
steady climb of our self-destruction,
the off-the-chart spike of our own undoing?

CONVERSATION WITH A FRIEND

Everything is serious now, in this time
of old age and plague, this time when even
Death loses count. Everything is serious,

even jokes, that all seem to end now with
a half-hearted *whatever* because even
punchlines are on the mat, wheezing,

losing consciousness. I try to laugh with
you, carry on a normal conversation, until
a kernel of panic and ambiguous anger

fires up in my gut, bangs the back
of my teeth, until my teeth give way
and the kernel becomes a skunk cannon,

a spray of vitriol and fear of dying gone
rancid from choking it down; six feet apart
will not be enough. You tell me how to be

scared in the proper way, because you're
terrified too and everyone's an expert now.
All the manuals are burning in the square,

even the flames afraid to cross each other.
Under a mask, I bend my face into what
I can still remember of a smile. We try

to ignore the TV, where peasants push
a wooden cart while their bored slavemaster
cracks his whip, calls *Bring out your dead!*

REWILDING

A hunter's moon lifts above treeless
bluffs east of the Missouri. A ribbon
of silver shimmers its way across
the water to the western bank, where

we're tucked in the river valley.
The wind is finally dying down.
Tent flaps settle like great primordial
wings. I call on ancestral genes, cell

memory, Akashic records, wood sprites—
whatever will help me start this fire
against the October cold. Crumpled
pages of the *Plain Talk* ignite, kindling

sparks, flames jump and lick split wood
I've balanced in a pyramid over the
kindling. Smoke tendrils shift, reach,
wrap me in their wild perfume.

Where shadows dip and glide in the
western bluffs behind us, coyotes begin
their chorus, call the pack to a kill.
Here by the dancing flames, Beloved,
        we open our throats and answer.

HUMMINGBIRD MOTH

after Eavan Boland

On a late May afternoon she appears,
Hemaris, bee-hawk moth, snowberry
clearwing. She is here, not having come

lazily along, but as a sudden apparition.
She is chimera—part heart-melting
hummingbird, her fantail waggling,

rolled tongue unfurled to dip into
bee balm, million bells, phlox,
and part nightmare, fringed antennae

searching, yellow cape of fur, scaled
wings nearly transparent. She
will stick her larvae to the underside

of honeysuckle leaves, leave her young
to drop on the grass, wrap themselves
in silk, wait for spring. I am elbow-deep

in a thicket of tomato vines, knees
clicking like cards on bike tires, when
her hovering stirs a vibration along

my spine. Like hers, my season here
is short. We will both beat our wings
to exhaustion, and when too soon

glorious adults emerge from torn
cocoons, we will fall down, she and I,
burrow beneath the leaf litter and sleep.

THE PALM READER: Fortune's Folly

The palm reader's assistant leads me
to a brocade chair. The table
is draped in silk, a red candle flickers
somewhere behind me, and I have
never in my life seen so much fringe.

The assistant lights another red candle
as a robed Marie-Annette floats
through heavy curtains, sits across
from me. *Give me your hands,* she says,
and pulls up her winged sleeves.

She takes hold of my fingers, flips
both hands palm up. She can't hide
the quick intake, the slight gasp.
She runs a fingernail along my love line.
You've been disappointed, she says, as if

I didn't already know. Isn't love always
disappointing, I think but keep
my replies to *I see,* or *You don't say.*
She bends my hands at the wrists,
says I will live into my 90s. More

disappointment, I think. She says
my heart is ruled by Saturn, leaving me
restless, unsatisfied. She tells me
about my lack of wealth, my poor
health, my fear of unraveling.

Your fate line will change soon,
she says. *A shift is coming.* I shift
in my chair. There, I think.
I pull back my hands, look at my fate
line and wait for it to change.

I feel the stale air leave my lungs
and drop $20 in her velvet box.
She and I look each other in the eye.
We both know everything she's said
was clear the moment I walked in.

THE DORMITION OF MOTHER

Like Mary, my mother was naïve
when at seventeen she married a sailor,
and at eighteen, when the first baby

came. She too trusted booming voices
that said hers was a life ordained—
formica dinette, wall-to-wall carpet,

dog tied in the yard, husband that would
stay. And like Mary, my mother was
never told about the rest, about life's

betrayals that hollowed her out, four
mewling kids who needed everything,
husband who skulked off with a stripper.

Let us hum softly, then, when at last
Mother, soothed by an inaudible choir
or slow dissolution of cell walls, sleeps.

Let us feast when the light we call *her*
spirals through the crown chakra or
pushes through the soles of her feet

or expands beyond the body's borders
to join the milky river of light that powers
the universe, light we call by many names.

Let her finally be all she meant to be or
nothing at all. Let her rest at last or ascend,
weightless as milkweed seed in a north wind.

Ghazal: WALKING ON THE EDGE OF NIGHT

after Agha Shahid Ali

We're most fully human on the cusp, the seed of night,
with pretense left behind to gather dust. Then comes the night.

You walk about when all the world's gone dark, when footsteps
tap Morse code in patterns meant just for the weary night.

Shadows move along a wall, stretch, point long bent
fingers toward the distant black, tricks of wanderlust at night.

Hypnotic glitter's net—stars, lake's surface, silver maple
leaves' flicker—you're caught in the moondust night.

From house vents, late-hour laundress scents—"soft rain,"
"sea breeze," "spring meadow," sudden gust of "summer night."

You keep to back alleys, where past lives tower in great heaps
of broken bikes, swing sets gone to rust. No play tonight.

Sizzle-pop and spit of snapping wires precedes a fire that
lights a street, melts someone's home to crust in dead of night.

The owl's silent glide, the moan of cats, the coyote's howl
harmonize with our despair or lust—the needs of night.

And what of you, Wanderer, creeping closer to the edge?
Will you let go, release your grip on morning, trust the night?

ST. JEANNE JUGAN

patron of poor old women

Shepherdess, spinner of wool and miracles,
even half blind you saw in every hoary face
Christ's disguise. Can you find him in me?

You, who refused the marriage bed of silk
and oils, who gave up your own plain bed
to women left on roadsides holding out

cups, you who spent decades begging for
alms, clothes, food, walls—for anything
to save disused and discarded old women.

St. Jeanne, bless me. Give me a quiet place
in your safehouse. I am disappearing now
in the greed of youth, that jealous fog.

Shine your muted light on me, little sister
of the poor. Let your compassion be a beacon
to cut through the grey, so for a few clear,
cloudless moments, I can be seen again.

THE FAT LADY: Baby Beulah Says Yes

Beulah said no to her father's backhand
across her eight-year-old face, that day
she chased the dog through the kitchen
and knocked over his beer. She said no

to the times he shook her or threw her
against a wall. She said no to her mother's
bruises, her turned back and vacant
mumbling, *be a good girl, mind Daddy.*

Beulah ate her anger. She said no
to the boys in junior high who offered
to pay for a feel, no when they held her
down anyway. She lived on Butterfingers

and French fries for months after that,
imagined each bite a rebellion, banner,
weapon. By eighteen, she was over
300 pounds, which didn't stop the drunk

who grabbed her in back of Bronco's.
She said no then, too. After that, she hid
Twinkies in shoe boxes, ate them at
night in the pitch black. She said nothing

to the other secretaries in the Mutual
Insurance pool when they asked,
Can you see your own muff? then
laughed and kept asking. By 35, Beulah

was almost 600 pounds. When she met
Frank at Safeway, and he asked if she
wanted to be a star—see *BABY BEULAH*
in lights every night, sit on a velvet

throne, wear rhinestones, eat prime rib
on stage, sing and play her violin,
decide for herself who could come back
to her wagon—Beulah said *YES.*

VULTURES

No, turkey vultures aren't the stunning
runway blondes. They're not the sweet
young brides or strutting boy-men
with their prancy flapflapflapping.

Turkey vultures are the grandmothers
of birdlife, avian housewives who
scrape dirty dishes, scrub floors,
mop around the toilet. They follow

behind us all, pick up shit we abandon
in heaps or toss from car windows or
leave in basements to fester, dead things
in corners that stink until they don't.

But in the evening when the work is done,
the dead and dying out of sight, they glide—
cathartes aura, "cleansing breeze"—
graceful, hypnotic, on invisible columns

of warm air. Great fingered wings
spread, dip or lift, steer in loose circles
above, bald heads tucked, watching.
Serene and patient, they wait for us.

SECOND CHANCE

The girl walked with purpose, barefoot between the dunes where a path had been pressed into the rough sand. She kept going past high tide's line of detritus or treasure—arms of jellyfish, Coke cans, shopping bags, a wool sock, bleached and brittle mollusk homes, their residents plucked by relentless hoodlum gulls. She walked on until the sand smoothed under the weight of water, then on until her feet blurred in a wave, on until the hem of her dress wicked up salt, on until she wore arm cuffs of seaweed, on until her sundress billowed out like a sail, tenting shoals of killifish, on until her hair caught a current and drifted into a halo around her disappearing crown. But Grandmother Moon was watching. She spit into the water, sent a wave big enough to toss the girl sputtering and cursing back onto the beach, where she would have to choke down another bite at the cherry.

HERMIT'S PRAYER

> *The bitterest time, the worst of all,*
> *Was that in which the summer sheen*
> *Cast a green luster on the wall*
> *That told of fields of lovelier green.*
>   *Emily Brontë*

Emily, let me fold my swollen,
fear-white knuckles in the hem of your
plain skirt. Drag me through these
crocheted bars to heathered moors
peaceful as the grave where I can sing
dirges, give myself a man's name,
swoon, faint from the holiness of desire.

Emily, you know the pain of openings
and closings. Help me to go out, to wander
past columned shadows, past crumbling
poisoned wells, past billowing spider silk
transparent and quivering, strung with
droplets like pearls, strung like a net
above spires of bright green grass.

THE FISH MAN: Neptune in the Coffee Shop

Sally puddle-jumps to keep her Keens dry,
        hops through the coffee shop door, sleigh bell
ringing above her. The counter is decked out
        in garland and red ribbons, an elf on the shelf
presses his face from inside a glass French press.

She gets her Americano and takes a far table
        near the fireplace, where no one will bother her.
She opens her laptop and is posting nasty comments
        on Facebook when the doorbell dings, an old man enters.
He leaves a trail of slime across the floor from door

to counter, orders Oolong. Sally's watching him,
        don't sit here don't sit here looping in her head.
He turns, eyeballs her, and heads straight for the table
        next to hers. The carnival's in town, she
remembers. Carnies give her the creeps. He smells

like dead fish, leans a rusty trident against the fireplace.
        All the paint has flaked off the giant fork's cracked
wooden pole, an old rake handle duct-taped to a
        hayfork head. One outside prong is missing,
worn to a nub. He sits down and blows on his tea.

He wears an oilcloth duster, and when he reaches
        for the Sweet 'N Low, Sally sees seaweed
and barnacles clinging to his thick wrist.
        His beard is green with algae, his face the color
of a ripe plum from baking in the sun. He has that

bulbous nose old alcoholics get. He drips seawater
        onto the coffee shop's beige carpet. Sally tries
to look without looking like she's looking. He reaches
        in his pocket and pulls out something. Several
pea-sized crabs come out too, clinging to his hand.

He shakes them off, they drop to the carpet, skitter away.
        He hands Sally what could be a business card.
It's soggy and looks like a wide fish scale. *NEPTUNE,*
        is all it says. He winks at her. Sally looks from his
outstretched hand to his face. She's breathless, like she's under

water, the air suddenly too thick. She doesn't take the card.
        She stuffs everything back in her backpack, leaves
her coffee and runs for the door. Neptune shrugs, crosses
        his legs, shakes out a newspaper, sips his tea.
Near the door, the long after-tone of a sleigh bell.

A GIFT

It's been a hard few years, so much to lose,
and I've been afraid to go out. This love
that works in me and feeds me, Beloved,
is all I can give you. It will have to do.

It spills out of me, like dust-weight seeds
that with some god's breath crack open,
germinate in you, until this love sends
rootsilk into every hidden corner of you.

I wasn't watching, or I would have
known how much you've needed such
a gift, caught as you've been by the wing
of your own sorrows, battered by regret,

fluttering against our losses. There's still
time for us. Let this love untangle us
from our barbed past, mend with its
soft reach every broken place in you,

give you strength enough to let go.
Listen to it hum, feel how it melts
on your tongue. Let it dissolve in you,
let it make you quake. And when

you've become all you can, when you
feel it vined around each bone and nerve,
when it blooms in the cave of your chest,
open yourself wide and give it away.

YOUR HANDS TELL ME GOODBYE

The night you died, Mother, we were
both exhausted—you so startled by it all,
slowly slipping down in the hospital
bed, and me half in a chair and half

bent over you, guardrail for a pillow.
When the morphine finally let you
breathe, you closed your eyes, and
I put myself to bed six feet away,

lullaby of your O2 generator singing
me into troubled sleep. I woke after
midnight, generator hissing, tubes
in a tangle on the floor where you

had somehow thrown them. There
you were, blankets shoved down
to your knees, eyes wide and fixed
on some invisible fascination, mouth

open as if asking me to look too, hands
resting on your stomach. Those hands.
They were already yellow as Grandma's
doilies, knuckles blue, nailbeds deep

purple. Even as I wept, I took a photo
to keep your hands in mine, hands that
before you slept held my face as
you said *I love you so,* one last time.

ECONOMY OF MOVEMENT

We must not waste a single muscle
contraction now, Beloved, reaching
for an onion, say, or bending to
pick up peeled golden beets that roll

onto the floor. We should hire
an efficiency expert to calculate
the proper pivot, lift height, and
speed needed for running

to the bathroom after an
unexpected laugh, or getting up
from our La-Z-Chairs to fetch
another fat-free ice cream bar

without letting blood rush
to our brains (we mustn't interrupt
with dizzy spells a smooth
glide to the kitchen table,

where our nightly pills form tiny
constellations on Aunt Elma's
tablecloth). We've been so frivolous,
so reckless with our movements—

bouncing on toboggans or horseback,
twisting around each other naked,
throwing balls for the dogs,
strumming ukuleles, dancing,

arms and legs all pinwheely.
Our movement storehouse echoes
as it empties, sluggish knees and
stretched tendons buckle and groan.

So let us economize now, Beloved,
dispense with dish-doing, dusting, mulching
of lawns. Let us hoard our dwindling motion,
save up for more dancing, more twisting.

THE TATTOOED LADY: Seeing Madame X for the First Time

When the robe comes off, you won't see
the rippled skin, fine lines or creases around
my eyes and lips. When the robe comes off,

I am Botticelli's *Venus, Le Rêve, Starry Night,*
veiled virgin. I am marble and canvas. You'll
watch (heart pounding, mouth agape) the

full moon glide across a midnight sky on my
thigh, count stars that fall into shadow between
my breasts, gasp as strange creatures splash

in the river of my neck. My arms will tell you
stories—girl on a swing, broken, still-hopeful
mother hanging sheets on a line. Girl alone

and lost, cityscape looming behind, every
window a dark, fanged mouth. On one leg
a flock of crows flies toward my ribs' cloudy

horizon. On the other leg a panther stalks
a sleeping doe and fawn. When I turn my back,
you'll be among the curved trees of Hoia forest,

its nightly ghosts pale, indistinct behind the black
bark. Flowering ivy twists from forehead to feet,
clings to itself. From everywhere, unblinking eyes

look back at you. What these bits of red
velvet hide! And when you are mesmerized,
scandalized, your wife at your elbow pulling,
know you've seen only what I let you see.

THRESHOLD

> *I'm a dweller on the threshold*
> *As I cross the burning ground*
> *Let me go down to the water*
> *Watch the great illusion drown*
>   *–Van Morrison*

On one side is a doctor's wife.
A lamb roast sizzles in the oven.
Limp pastel daisies wilt on linen
napkins in an antiseptic kitchen.
Her eyebrows form perfect
inverted Vs. Highrise, box-blonde
hair sets off a constant smile,
her white eyelet apron barely
brushing each dinner guest.

On the other side is a madwoman
dancing down an unlit alley,
black choir robe tied at the waist
with clothesline. Her cowboy
boots grind broken bottles
into gravel. She spins, dips,
sings *blackbird has spoken*
like the first bird, disappears
into the dark, a vanishing angel.

I'm on the threshold, slower,
more careful now, a beaded
purse suspended from my
wrist, Fool tarot cool and slick
in my other hand. I'm afraid
to move, afraid of falling, framed
in fog and moonlight that reflect
just now off bleach-blonde hair
and the burnt tip of an angel wing.

MY DARKENING WINDOW

I still see you some evenings, but only
in fragments now, fractals of you
still-framed in memory or imprinted

on the backs of my eyes, I can't tell
which, layered and uncertain like
watching seabirds through the beveled

edge of a pebbled window. Or reflected
in a mirror, its silver creased, cracked,
chipping away. You seem so close

I whisper to you anyway—*Help me!*
How can you leave me orphaned,
suspended in this unforgiving air?

Night moves in, wraps me in its cool
embrace. You retreat again and again,
my darkening window closing.

IN DEFENSE OF WINTER

In the sudden, perfect quiet, people with their constant
nervous noise retreat inside. Houses are shuttered,
sealed, blanketed. Traffic slows to an occasional hushed
slushing past, but even then, car windows are rolled up
against the wind and the human barrage of *talktalktalk*,
the radio's *thumpcrashwhine* safely sealed away.

Blue and bitter cold flushes skin with blood, numbs
fingers, pinches eartips. Shivering reminds us we are
animals, our bodies know what to do. Winter purifies,
preserves, resets us on its clean slate. Back inside it's
warm, winter's contrast, survival's temporary truce.
Breath turns brush on icy windows, every surface a canvas.

Into the jeweled night! We don layers, boots and masks,
walk out in the snowdrift dark. We meet one other
dogwalker who keeps to her side of the street, gives
a quick gloved wave, moves on. All is reverie, moving
contemplation of shapes and signs in crushed diamonds,
moonlight and starlight refracted in a landscape of prisms.

The Wheel of living and dying turns. Winter freezes
all to glass, suspends and wraps in snow or shatters
our sorrows, failures, decay and detritus, plans
that take us nowhere. But prairie people know
rebirth only comes from death, and winter's
death is tender, peaceful, still with hope.

THE HOUSE OF GLASS: All the Little Hammers

On the back of the lot, past the Hook-A-Duck,
behind the High Striker where muscled
young men flex and strut, at the edge
of the rented pasture is the House of Glass.

In the dark tent, colored spotlights flicker
and glint on glass panels, each threaded
through its center and held up with pins
and rods from crisscrossed ceiling wires.

When on the last night of the carnival
the flap opens and light leaks in, the whole
tent is an enchanted wind chime, panels
turning, clinking as they touch each other.

From each panel one weathered carny
looks out, wisps of white hair flying beyond
the glass. Some are stooped, half blind,
but all plod through familiar routines—

counting tickets, taping electrical cords,
folding laundry, knotting sequins, salting
stew, painting numbers on rubber ducks,
mucking out the elephant wagon.

As the panels slowly rotate, the glass people
work. Sometimes they wave to each other
until sideways, they disappear, come back
around. Now and then a sudden gust

whips through the tent and a panel shatters,
blown into a tent pole or a friend, and Jerome,
smaller than a toddler, ambles in with a push
broom, sweeps shards under the tent skirt.

Replacement panels are harder to come by
these days. Outside, a line of curious kids
still titters about double-jointed Tiana. Each
has a coin, a little hammer in their pocket.

Ghazal: DREAM OF THE WORLD

The world is inhospitable when past your prime,
prime being 25 or less, today's sweet dream of age.

Doors are made for muscled arms, rings for unlined hands,
beds six feet off the floor to seem more stage

than sanctuary. Where once a slower gait, a stoop, earned
respect, or sympathy at least, now a semi-clean cage

staffed by eye-rolling children—the *home*, it's called—
opens wide its maw to bite us in, we now deemed the age

of uselessness. And in a corner by a window, we watch
the birds, tap fingers to a ticking clock. We, sepia pages

torn from cast-off books. Wanderer, stand up. Make
noise. Wear the bustier. The world is your dream too. Rage.

THOSE NIGHTS WHEN YOU COME BACK

On nights when the veil is thin and you come
back to haunt me, Mother, in spite of sage,

candles, turned-down portraits, covered
mirrors, I back trance-like out of the

kitchen to hide in the hall closet. The dogs
howl, always impressed by your slow

motion wavering, as if you were bad TV
reception and all we had to do was fiddle

with the rabbit ears. You want to steer this
ship again, unconvinced you've gone beyond.

When I peek out the door, there you are
shaking your finger at me, eyebrows

cocked, mouthing a soundless command.
I want to run away, or run into your arms,

to hold you or run through you, but I wait,
still obedient, until you wisp and falter,

vacuumed back through the curtain. I finish
drying dishes, already missing you again.

PLAIN LOVE SONG

Shake off the glitter, don't
be dazzled by cupidy arrows.

Love is not in the heart. It's in
your slow, steady hands, Beloved,

that put things right after
a thunderstorm, your strong

back that hoes a tomato bed,
in the way you stoop for dogplay

or bend to sweep up pieces
of my broken coffee cup.

It's in your stomach muscles
twisted into braids on days

when I can't find my way,
in your patient calling, calling,

until I can breathe again.
It's in the watching, waiting,

in your unshakeable faith
that I'll come back.

CAILLEACH FEASA

After Mother died, I took my rightful place,
cailleach feasa, hag witch of the house.
Where once I'd kept my spells under wraps,

now I wave my wooden spoon, wandlike
and unashamed, my hair unpinned and still
hysterical red, lashing across my brow.

I have earned my cauldron, its daily brew
a strange new stew of pennyroyal, men's
stiff gym socks, lock of fine white hair.

In a Sasquatch hoodie and pashmina, with
a suffer-no-shit, cocked-eyebrow scowl,
I stir the pot—mashup of *Diving Into the*

Wreck and *Daddy* for an incantation.
Out in the garage, you adapt, Beloved, learn
when it's safe to come inside, and when,

if I'm working my magic, hurling curses,
feeding the fire, you're wiser to stay where
you are, hammering something, anything.

THE LAST POEM I'LL WRITE

I should etch this poem in the glass
        of your eye. This, the last
                poem I'll write.

Each time you stare
        at a horizon of bluestem,
                wheat, sunflowers,

or into a cloudless July sky,
        or down at the still surface
                of the lake you'll hear me call

Beloved! my voice suddenly
        vibrato, a ripple of prairie wind
                or a restless bluegill.

We are a book of devotion, nearly
        complete, we'll leave unfinished.
                Don't be afraid to open your eyes.

THE MIDWAY: Shuttering

When the carnival shutters for the night,
iron gates pulled and chained and all
the clowns long since snoring
in cartoon honks and train whistles,
I walk the lane, pulling plugs on a map
of lights that swings in the night breeze.

The carousel is quiet now—sunbleached
horses, elephants, sea serpents, frozen
in the day's final undulations. The
Fun House too is dark, great carved
doorways like gaping yawns. Sideshow
stars settle in, their teeth in bedside jars.

There is so much peace on the Midway
tonight. I've left behind the nightly
intrigues in the neighborhoods of my
youth for this quieter circus, for the
hermitage of my wagon, its paint chipped
and fading. I've traded my girl's baubles—

high heels, lipstick, plunging necklines,
pushup bras, hair spray, tantrum & euphoria,
traded my apron and spatula, my briefcase
and watch with its relentless ticking—for a
velvet chair, a book with its tatty cover, hot
tea and honey, these muted colors of fall.

RELEASE

In the un-earthing,
when whatever remains of us
is released from our crumbling

bodies, perhaps our sparks will
unfold wings of silver-white light
and free at last we will, for a time,

ride the grey horizon until we lift,
melt into the star-sequined dark,
until our lights are brief pin-pricks

in the velvet black and we, pure
joy. Perhaps back down here, still
heavy with earth, some will look up,

button up tight their coats of longing
and grief, quiet their hands in deep
pockets and walk on into the night.

ACKNOWLEDGMENTS

This book is dedicated to my parents with love, gratitude, forgiveness, and release.

With love and thanks to Allen for absolutely everything; to our children, grandchildren, and furry and feathered companions for their love and patience; to my brothers for their constant support; and to the Women Poets Collective for their insights and generosity in helping me shape this collection.

My thanks to the editors of the following publications for including poems from this collection:

Banyan Review, "Snow Beasts," "What I Try to Believe," "The Last Poem I'll Write"
The Briar Cliff Review, "Hummingbird Moth"
Final Girl Anthology, Porkbelly Press, "The Bearded Lady: Un-becoming"
Green Elephant, Scurfpea Press, "St. Muirgen"
Live Encounters, "Cusp of Morning," "Release," "The Time Before"
O'Bheal 5-Word Challenge Anthology (Ireland), "Bathing Mother" (Top 10 Short List), "Caught" (First Place)
Pasque Petals, "The Open Sea," "She is the Kind of Person Who," "Those Nights When You Come Back," "Wild Winter"
Poetry Ireland Review, "Cailleach Feasa"
Quartet, "Rewilding"
SWWIM Every Day, "Walking on the Edge of Night"
Tangled Serenity, Scurfpea Press, "Long Track Home," "Threshold"

MARCELLA REMUND is originally from Omaha, Nebraska, transplanted to South Dakota. Her work has appeared in *The Briar Cliff Review, Jabberwock, Poetry Ireland Review, Pasque Petals, Banyan Review, Sheila-Na-Gig, Quartet,* and other journals and anthologies. She is the author of four poetry books, *The Sea is My Ugly Twin, The Book of Crooked Prayer, Hysterian,* and *Stroke, Stroke* all from Finishing Line Press. Find more information at www.marcellaremund.com.

www.ingramcontent.com/pod-product-compliance
Lightning Source LLC
Chambersburg PA
CBHW030056170426
43197CB00010B/1551